AFFIRM

&

NURTURE

A New Look at 12 Steps

Mark T. Scannell

GASSCANN PUBLISHERS
Minneapolis, Minnesota

ISBN 978-0-9966511-5-8 (softcover)

Cover design by Carson Creative.

GASSCANN PUBLISHERS
4556 18th Avenue South
Minneapolis, Minnesota 55407
gasscann@bitstream.net

DEDICATION

Among all of the supportive people and communities that have helped me understand the power of affirmation, hope, and the wisdom of The Twelve Steps, I especially dedicate this book to my wife Elaine and the 12-Step group I have been a member of for almost thirty years.

To Elaine. I am most grateful that our paths first crossed some fifty-five years ago, and we have journeyed the road of life for all these years together. I am grateful for your support and love all this time and sticking by me on the good days as well as the hard days. I have learned from you how each of us is called to be the artist of our lives; we are called to be creative. And I came to experience the power of affirmation through you, along with an ability to continue to hope. Thank you!

To the members of my SAA 12-Step men's group. Thank you to the many men who were part of this group when I joined, have been members over the years, and are members now. Through all of you, I have learned the wisdom of The Twelve Steps and, from the ways that you welcomed me when I was struggling, how we continue to welcome people today. I couldn't have even thought of writing this book without you all. Thank you!

I am a grateful man.

CONTENTS

INTRODUCTION / PROLOGUE

I embarked upon writing this book on the Twelve Steps with some temerity. I am well aware that many others have reflected on and shared their awarenesses after Bill W introduced the Steps in the 1930s. The Twelve Steps have stood the test of time for almost ninety years. I see that longevity as a true sign of their being a source of wisdom for people in our healing and recovery.

Writing these reflections from a positive perspective on the Twelve Steps has been something I considered for a while, and I finally decided that it's now or never. I am aware that I am growing older, and I believe I am being called to offer this perspective.

The thoughts I share in this book arise out of the insights of others who have written about their experiences, and many of their reflections are included in the Bibliography. Other sources are my own experiences in a 12-Step group for almost thirty years. The Twelve Steps and the SAA group I discovered in Minneapolis became, and continue to be, a lifeline, helping me as I confront my addictions and seek help for my recovery.

A learning that came to me very early in my experience is that the Twelve Steps come most alive in conversations shared in these gatherings. The struggles shared, as well as the breakthroughs experienced, are the bases for the bonding and support that are so necessary for recovery.

I have learned much from working the Steps individually as well as from listening to the experiences of others in the group I attend. Key parts of my life experience are being raised a Catholic as well as becoming a Catholic priest. Biblical stories have always spoken to me, and I include some along the way in this book.

A story in the fifth chapter in the Gospel of Luke speaks of a paralyzed person whose friends believed that if they could bring their friend to Jesus, Jesus would heal him. They carried their friend on a bed to where Jesus was teaching, and the room where Jesus was teaching was full. The friends were not deterred! They carried their paralyzed friend up onto the roof, and lowered him into the middle of the crowd in front of where Jesus was teaching.

"When Jesus saw their faith" (Luke 5:20), the man was healed. Jesus had responded to their faith.

In this story, the paralysis of the man can be seen as a symbol of his loss of faith. His friends believed in Jesus and carried their friend to Jesus, and Jesus healed the person.

This story speaks directly to me of my experiences in the 12-Step group I attend. We need the help and support of others to find healing and recovery. At times I need to be carried; and other times, I am part of a group that carries someone else. Recovery is always a two-way street—we all need the help and support of others.

I have learned much from "working" the Steps and listening to how others have worked the Steps. I have also wrestled with the Steps. I have especially wrestled and struggled with what I have experienced as a somewhat negative tone to the Steps—a sense of focusing on the wrongs we have done, the amends we can make to people we have harmed, and how we must promptly admit when we are wrong.

I do not disagree with these actions or their importance in our recoveries. But in this book, I focus more on the opposite side of the coin in our awarenesses—upon how vital it is to AFFIRM the positives in our recoveries: the good things we've done, the people we've helped and those who have helped us, as well as awarenesses of the reasons we are grateful.

As I walk through the Twelve Steps in this book, I share my rendition of the Steps in a way that emphasizes the more-positive dimensions. In doing so, I realize I'm taking a risk that some may feel offended. My goal is not to offend anyone. I offer this book, and my own positive renditions of the Steps, to hopefully bring greater awareness to these more-positive dimensions of recovery. In contributing my reflections on the Twelve Steps, I hope that it will lead to more dialogues about the Steps that will help anyone whether they are working the Steps alone or working along with others.

I know that perfection does not exist in this world, and human awarenesses and insights continue as people share their experiences and learn with and from others. At the same time, I love to play with words. I have studied Latin, and I think of myself as something of a wordsmith.

The Latin root for the word "learning" is the verb *disco*. So I suggest that a "disciple," from this perspective, is always a learner. To be a follower of any tradition—whether it be a philosophy, a way of living, or even the Twelve Steps—is an invitation to continue to learn and share experiences. Any tradition where there is no room for exchanges and changes is basically dead. Change is an infallible sign of life!

WE ARE CALLED TO BE LIFELONG LEARNERS!

So many people have influenced me in my life and in my recovery—I realize the older we get, the more people have influenced me and us. I am grateful to all of those people—too many to name individually. Here I want to say thank you again to all of you and them.

A few of the people were especially helpful to me with this book include Dr Ira Progoff, who besides teaching me the Intensive Journal method of journaling, taught me much about spirituality. Brené Brown's research and reflections on shame—such a large part of the world of addictions—contributed much to my wrestling with the shame that I experienced through my addictive behaviors as well as walking with others as they deal with their shame.

I also am grateful for Erik Erikson's pioneering work around how we develop from children to adults and for posing this development in terms of the challenges we face at each period (stage) of our development.

As we face these challenges, we usually struggle. Part of recovery, then, is accepting both the successes we have had as well as the failures. Erikson's framework is helpful in conceptualizing where we have come from and where we are going. He has given us a roadmap to discover where we have been and are in our journeys.

To provide quick overview of how I will proceed in this book, each chapter begins with a statement of the Step/s being discussed (some of the Steps are treated together as twins). In some, I include my own additions to the Step/s. I then reflect on each Step.

The first chapter includes some terms that I see as fundamental to understanding what I present on the Steps. In the Epilogue, I raise some topics for further reflection in the area of recovery from addictions.

Throughout this book, I invite you to bring along your experiences. Each chapter concludes with Reflection Questions to hopefully stimulate learning and discussion. I hope these will encourage you to think about your experiences as well as share your reflections with others.

Thank you for jumping on board and coming along for this journey with me about the Twelve Steps. I am always open to your sharing your feedback with me—suggestions, questions, and areas where you might see things differently. Dialogue is a valuable and important way we learn and continue to learn.

I invite each of us to AFFIRM the positive wherever we experience positivity in our lives and NURTURE the same in the lives of others as well. I believe that we will grow and develop more easily when we are working from the positives rather than only from the negatives.

CHAPTER I

SETTING THE STAGE: A GLOSSARY OF TERMS

As I begin this reflection on the Twelve Steps, I thought it might be helpful to mention some of the sources and some terms that I use in this book. My wife and I enjoy attending plays at various theaters in town. We know that the stage (as the setting where the play is enacted) is an important component of every play.

Here I "set the stage" for what you will find in this book.

AFFIRM THE POSITIVE AND NURTURE HOPE TO ADDRESS ADDICTIVE BEHAVIORS

The idea and reality of affirming the positive and nurturing hope is the theme of this book in addressing addictive behaviors. This is about our ability to say "Yes" to another person, and to ourself, and to again and again and again choose the positive over the negative.

Affirming the positive is an ongoing choice in our lives. The word "affirm" in close to the word "accentuate," which recalls for me the song, "Ac-Cent-Tchu-Ate the Positive," written by Johnny Mercer and Harold Arlen. Some of the lyrics are: *"You've got to ac-cent-tchu-ate the positive, eliminate the negative and latch onto the affirmative, and don't mess with Mister In-between."*

The message of the song feels very apropos in the presence of so much negativity around the world—wars, polarizations, conflicts and divisions, to name just a few negatives in our lives. As the song goes on to say:

"Ya got to spread joy to the maximum, bring gloom down to the minimum, and have faith, or pandemonium's liable to walk upon the scene."

Doesn't that sound familiar—like what we find happening around us so often, and what is needed in so many places?

Along with affirming and accentuating the positive, an important dimension for us to address is the essential need to NURTURE our hopes and not give up—or give in—to a deep kind of hopelessness.

An ongoing battle for many of us is between the desire to hope and a temptation to give up. These two themes are the backdrop and inspiration for this look at the Twelve Steps.

Addictive behaviors are often a way to medicate our pain and discomfort. Addictions, such as drinking, using drugs, overeating, pornography, and overworking, might work for a while. But their impact is usually to isolate us from others, which naturally becomes a fertile ground for more addictive behaviors.

I strongly believe that belonging to a community or communities is the fertile ground for recovery. We all search for communities where we can find support—the support that encourages us to see the positives of life and not just the negatives or challenges. Even when we want to remain hopeful and positive, we may be feeling heartbroken by the many harsh challenges we have had to endure.

Some of the positives we must NURTURE are the abilities to see our own gifts and talents as well as our abilities to change and grow. This is hard to do alone!

We all need the support of others.

The Twelve Steps created by Bill W and Doctor Bob, back in 1935, have a solid tradition and an impressive track record in helping people recover from addiction. The Steps initially focused on helping people recover from alcoholism. Over the years, they have also become a valuable foundation for helping people with *all forms* of addiction.

My taking a step to reword and amplify a few of the Steps might be seen by some as committing some sort of heresy. Change, however, is a sign of life, and my intention here is to present the Steps in a new way that will help us to strongly AFFIRM the positives in our lives and further NURTURE hope in all of us.

ERIK ERIKSON'S STAGES OF DEVELOPMENT

A framework of polarities that caught my imagination many years ago was created by psychologist Erik Erikson. He described the struggles we all face in seeking to develop and grow into creative and nurturing adults who can and will contribute to society. He presents his framework in the form of specific struggles between two opposites at each stage of development.

Affirming positives and nurturing hope are always a struggle between the opposites he describes. Below are his eight stages summarized in simple terms with some added words bolded in **[brackets]**, plus **two more** stages I suggest including based upon my own decades of experiences with the Twelve Steps and it relationship with our life struggles throughout life as described by Erikson.*

Erickson expresses well the struggles we face as we grow up and decide who we want to be and what we will do.

However, I do not see the need to limit each struggle to a specific time period in life. No need to tie those down. Many of these struggles can stretch across more than one period in our lives. For example, as most people can attest, the struggle between intimacy and isolation is ongoing at *all* stages of adulthood. As we grow and progress in recovery, we are always dealing with the need to make choices between the opposites of our experiences.

I added **Hope** to integrity as this reflects another way to express integrity, which includes honesty, reliability, uprightness—the behavior features that keep us focused on hope and joy rather than despair. I added **creativity** to generativity because creativity speaks more about my own experiences of positivity and concern for others. The two added stages are also vital to the whole experience of recovery.

STAGES OF DEVELOPMENT

Trust vs. Mistrust (infancy)

Autonomy vs. Shame/Doubt (toddler)

Initiative vs. Guilt (preschool-age)

Industry vs. Inferiority (school-age)

Identity vs. Role Confusion (adolescence)

*** Courage vs. Fear (adolescence)**

Intimacy vs. Isolation (young adulthood)

Generativity **[Creativity]** vs. Stagnation (mid-adult)

Integrity **[Hope]** vs. Despair (older adulthood)

*** Gratitude vs. Ungratefulness (adult years)**

Courage is certainly necessary to confront our addictions and choose recovery. A regular practice of expressing **gratitude** and giving thanks are necessary for developing a healthy life on all levels. I addressed more about the importance and impact of expressing gratitude in my book on adding Gratitude to the Serenity Prayer.

RELIGION AND SPIRITUALITY

An ongoing issue often heard in relation to the Twelve Steps is a criticism that the Steps presume that a "religious" world view is required in order to achieve sobriety. Certainly my own background prescribed a "religious" world view.

I grew up in and continue to be part of a religious structure, the Catholic Church. I was raised Catholic on the west side of Chicago in the 1940s and '50s. I attended Catholic schools—from grammar school, junior high, high school, and two years of college at the University of Notre Dame.

All of these schools were deeply Catholic, and each was very traditional in how the Catholic religion was presented. When I then entered a Catholic community of priests and brothers, the Dominican Order, I spent seven years studying philosophy and theology in preparation for ordination to the priesthood in 1969. All through the 1960s, changes had begun to take place in the Catholic Church that made the Church much more flexible in some areas. This shift was very appealing to me.

I brought all these experiences of religion with me as I entered my first 12-Step SAA (Sex Addicts Anonymous) meeting in 1995. I was confused by the usage in some parts of the Twelve Steps that sometimes referred to "a God of our understanding" and, at other times, referred to a "Higher Power."

As I continued in this all-male group for a longer period of time, I heard men describe their struggles with God as well as the language used for God. Some of the men had had difficult experiences with a Church or a member of the clergy, or they were raised in a family without any tradition of God or Church. For some, "God language" brought lots of baggage.

Over time, I became more comfortable with the use of the term Higher Power in the Twelve Steps. Higher Power is a more inclusive term, open to more people. As a concept, Higher Power lacks the baggage that can come at times with the word "God."

I see God as "one of" my Higher Powers. I will explain in more detail about this important aspect of the Twelve Steps as I review the work of each step. Suffice it to say that I see the Twelve Steps not as a religion, and that it has everything to do with our individual spiritualities.

The Steps provide a methodology for people to become open to support from others and receive help without having to join a specific religion or church. The Twelve Steps are open to people of different religious traditions and spiritual paths.

I am welcome as a Catholic, and I enjoy welcoming others who are of this tradition as well as other traditions. I see 12 Step meetings as a kind of big tent that has room for everyone—needed so much today!

So then, what is important in relation to 12-Step groups?

The only requirement for membership is a desire to stop one's addictive behaviors, whatever they might be. The Twelve Steps present a spiritual outlook on recovery from addictions, not a religion.

That is a crucial distinction.

RESILIENCE

In my 2019 book, *Resilience: The Ability to Rebound from Adversity,* I described developing resilience as an important goal (and necessity) in recovery. Seeking recovery and maintaining sobriety are a profound challenge, and adversities are part of our recovery journeys.

We live in a challenging world, and the ability to bounce back from adversities and challenges as well as the ability to prepare for the challenges that life brings our way in every aspect of our lives are an invaluable tool. The Twelve Steps provide a path for developing resilience so that we are able to rebound from the mistakes we have made along the way in our lives as well as express gratitude for the support we have received.

COMMUNITY

Community is a most obvious and critical aspect of working the Twelve Steps recovery path from addiction. This awareness was strengthened after the Surgeon General of the United States issued a Report in May 2023, stating that loneliness is an epidemic in this country. He concluded that one of every two Americans is experiencing loneliness and disconnection. I found this figure astounding, frightening, and very challenging. The Surgeon General naming loneliness as an epidemic sounded much like COVID—and the resulting isolation that affected all Americans, including myself.

This report has enormous repercussions for addiction and for recovery. As we know all too well, addictive behaviors flourish in isolation—which is what loneliness and disconnection are all about. So much widespread loneliness and disconnection make finding communities in our lives a greater challenge. Community is an even more important reality when there is so much disconnection.

What is community then?

One of my wisdom figures, Jesus Christ, said, "Where two or three are gathered in my name, I am there among them." (Matthew 18:20).

I am struck that it only takes two or three for Jesus (or Higher Power) to show up!

A community is any group more than me! I plus one other can be a community just as well as you and another can be a community. Community is ultimately about quality, not quantity! Our 12-Step groups are important communities in helping us to recover from addictions.

An important insight came to me from a rather eccentric professor I had as I was preparing to become a priest. One day he said that he would like to share another slant on community. He said that *com* in Latin means "with," and the Latin noun *munus* means "task." He suggested, from those roots, that a community needs a focus as well as a task to stay alive and thrive. That means taking time to talk with each other about the dynamics of our groups and remind each other and ourselves about what we are trying to accomplish. This theme of community will emerge again and again as we reflect further on each of the Twelve Steps.

TRAUMA

Much is written these days about the connection between traumatic experiences and addiction. Trauma comes from a Greek word *traumatikos*, meaning wound. All of us (including myself) have experienced traumas of some sort. Dr. Bessel van der Kolk, the psychiatrist and best-selling trauma research author, details the posttraumatic stress experienced by women and men who have been abused as children in their families.

I was traumatized as a young boy growing up in the Catholic Church. The ways in which morality and sexuality were presented and connected with sin, guilt, and shame really frightened me. In an important book on this subject, *Trauma and the 12 Steps*, by Jamie Marich, the author connects traumas with addictions, explaining how traumas create pain for us, and addiction often becomes a way to medicate our pain. She offers two important qualities for 12-Step groups to provide a welcoming environment for victims of abuse: safety and flexibility.

I find those qualities very challenging to those of us who belong to 12-Step groups. I wonder . . .

Are we creating safe places needed for all the people who are part of the group?

And are we flexible to listen and welcome members who are struggling with shame and judgments that we have each also carried?

Do our own shame and judgments get in the way of that challenge?

Everyone who belongs to a 12-Step group can benefit from the advice and support offered in this book.

THE CURSE OF PERFECTIONISM

In preparation for diving into the Twelve Steps, I will name a topic that comes up in each chapter: something I call the "Curse of Perfectionism." To some degree—whatever our background and experiences—all of us have grappled with trying to meet some unattainable goal: to be perfect in some way. The societies to which we belong continue to assert the importance of striving to be perfect—having the most money, the highest grades in school, never making mistakes, etc.

The obvious fallacy here is that perfection does not exist in this world! All of us are imperfect, and we all make mistakes.

From my experience in struggling with my addictions as well as listening to others talk about their own, the desire to be perfect is very much alive and well and is often a contributing factor to our continuing to struggle with our addictions.

Each chapter in this book ends with some Reflection Questions. I used this format in each of my prior books, and I use them again for a variety of reasons. I hope the questions will help the reader reflect upon their own life experiences and learn more from them.

True learning often happens best when people share their awarenesses and experiences with others. I hope that the Reflection Questions will lead to dialogues with others about the topics and messages at the heart of this book.

Then it's time to dive into Step 1!

REFLECTION QUESTIONS

1. How do you affirm yourself and others? What actions are affirming of yourself and others?

2. Where do you find community these days? Do you feel you belong there?

3. What nurtures your sense of hopefulness these days?

CHAPTER II

STEP 1

STEP 1

We admitted we were powerless over our addictive behaviors[1]—that our lives had become unmanageable.

Step 1 parallels Erik Erikson's Stages of Development when we are experiencing inferiority, confusion, isolation, and despair. Despair is another word for hopelessness in Erikson's Stages.

Is there anything more depleting than feeling powerless?

We have so many possible sources of feeling powerless these days—feeling overwhelmed and unable to see anything positive or hopeful in the current situations we face. I can feel so

[1] The original wording focused on alcohol. Now the Twelve Steps apply to all addictions.

overwhelmed watching the news on television, feeling very powerless, scared, and sad about such large issues in the world, such as disasters, war, and widespread suffering, that I do not know how to have an impact.

We can also feel powerless when we have slipped in our programs to remain sober, or whatever be our addictions. Life these days throws us curve balls that lead us to feel powerless and often hopeless. These feelings and experiences can lead us to act out our addictions. And enough feelings of powerlessness can lead us to deeper feelings of hopelessness.

Another word that jumps out at me in Step 1 is "admitted." Any time we make an admission about any important aspect of our life, whether a success or failure, we are taking a risk. We aren't always sure how another person will interpret or judge what we say. Any admission takes courage, because we often fear how others will respond to what we share. The use of "admitted" to begin Step 1 suggests and reinforces the idea that it will take courage to work the Steps. And I have found that to be very true!

Step 1 also speaks of acknowledging the unmanageability that is part of our lives. Powerlessness and unmanageability often go hand in hand.

When we feel powerless, we can feel that our life has become unmanageable. And whenever we are experiencing unmanageability, we are also feeling powerless. They go together—just like the old horse-and-carriage metaphor. I also think that when we experience powerlessness and unmanageability, there is not something wrong with us or a reason to feel shame. When the events of today lead us to feel powerless, the question becomes: what can we do with these feelings? That really opens us to working the rest of the Steps.

Some examples of powerlessness and unmanageability include the inability to find a job that produces enough money to live comfortably, such as schoolteachers who are facing whether they can continue to teach and be able to afford the normal expenses of raising a family. Another example is the fear that arises if we live in a neighborhood marked by violence and feeling unsafe. Isolation and disconnections can come with aging and facing the loss of family members and friends. These and many, many other examples contribute to why many of us are feeling powerless and unmanageable, as well as lonely and disconnected, as discussed in the previous chapter, leaving us feeling hopeless and desperate.

When focusing on Step 1 and each of the other Steps, some

have noticed and commented that the most significant word that appears in all the Steps is "WE!" Recovery and resilience begin with a move out of "I" and finding a "WE," meaning the communities that can be a source of support and help. Life is difficult if you go it alone!

Remember: you never have to!

Another aspect of the word "admitted" is the *opposite* of denial or lying. To admit a failing or weakness is very difficult against the backdrop of the many messages from all over that are as pervasive as air we breathe (such as perfection, as mentioned). We are tempted to not share our weaknesses or failures and to hide the addictions we are struggling with in order to hide our pain and powerlessness. Telling the truth about (admitting) what is going on means exercising courage and taking the risk to ask for support and help.

I vividly remember the night I attended my first SAA meeting. I was filled with anxieties and fears that evening!

Who and what will I find there in that room?

What will I say about myself?

How will I explain what led me to that group?

What will they think of me?

Will I be welcome?

But such fears and anxieties can leave us stuck, unable to do what we need and want to do.

Gratefully I was welcomed by the members of the group that evening, and over time I gradually began to feel at home with them. Little did I know that I was working Step 1 that first evening! I took a risk to show up, and I was certainly very grateful to be welcomed and accepted.

Looking back upon that night and continuing to work Step 1, I found that some life experiences can all-too-easily thrust us right back into feeling powerless again. So, I have begun to feel and try to NURTURE some sense of empowerment. As a result, my life is a little more manageable by working the Steps and being involved in a supportive 12-Step group.

What I have experienced—and this is an introduction to Steps 2 and 3—is the power of a community, a WE that has helped me continue to admit when I am feeling powerless. What is also important here is also hearing others share where they are powerless—I am not alone in this boat, as others are with me as well.

In another wordsmithing example, the word "companion" comes from two Latin words—*com* meaning "with," and "*panion*" from the Latin word *panis* meaning "bread."

When we look at companion from this perspective then, companions are people who feed each other and are fed by each other. I often feel hungry, needing to be fed. I sometimes forget that I also have food to share with others who are hungry.

This hunger feeling reminds me of the story in the Gospel of Matthew (14:13-21), where a crowd has gathered to listen to Jesus, and his disciples remind Jesus that the people have been there a long time and are hungry. There doesn't seem to be enough food to feed everyone.

Jesus responds rather blandly with something like "feed them," which was seemingly easier said than done. The disciples respond that the only food available is that of a young boy with a few fish and some bread. The story speaks of Jesus blessing these items, and the result was enough to feed the entire huge crowd with much left over.

How was this possible? An explanation for this "miracle" that has always appealed to me, and I can't remember where I heard it, was this—simply that when others saw the young boy sharing what he had, they all began to share what they had. And the result was that all were fed with much left over. This wonderful interpretation suggests that, when we share what might feel meager and others do the same, we are all fed, with much left over. This resonates with how I often feel by way of abundance at 12-Step meetings; I always receive much more than what I give! I receive an abundance of wisdom, care, and support!

I have found many companions in my 12-Step group. I have been nourished by them as they remind me that I don't have to be perfect.

Such as atmosphere allows us to admit we are powerless and that our lives have become unmanageable. I hope you have also found such groups that have helped you to admit your struggles. They truly AFFIRM and NURTURE our lives and our HOPE!

REFLECTION QUESTIONS

1. What experiences leave you feeling powerless and feeling your life is unmanageable?

2. Do you have places and communities—companions—where and with whom you can share your powerlessness and unmanageability and find support and where you can be you?

3. What struggles do you face in admitting what is really happening in your life?

CHAPTER III

STEPS 2 & 3

STEP 2

We came to believe that a Power greater than ourselves could restore us to sanity.

STEP 3

We made a decision to turn our wills and our lives over to the care of our Higher Powers[2] as we understood our Higher Powers.

Here I treat these two Steps as twins. I mentioned in Setting the Stage, I prefer the term "Higher Power" instead of "God," because Higher Power is a more-inclusive term.

---

[2] The original wording used "God" instead of "Higher Powers."

I name one of my Higher Powers as God. You may notice that I use inclusive language throughout in this book, for example, humankind being more inclusive than mankind.

Continuing in this vein while reflecting upon Higher Power and the place of Higher Power in the Twelve Steps, I came upon a statement by Ernie Kurtz, who has written many books on recovery. In his book *Not God: A History of Alcoholics Anonymous*, he concludes that anyone or anything can be our Higher Power (as long as it isn't ourselves).

His statement came like a bolt of lightning to my understanding of Higher Power. From this perspective, then, I can have multiple Higher Powers—God, a partner, a sponsor, a group, even a value such as honesty, etc. This concept of multiple Higher Powers lends itself to a more pragmatic approach when you consider what really works for you in envisioning a Higher Power or Powers that can help you achieve and maintain sobriety.

As I reflected further upon this idea of multiple Higher Powers, I was struck by the awareness that this is very much in keeping with what the Catholic Church teaches about God. If someone desires to become a Catholic, the person is encouraged to join a local Catholic Church.

Clearly this is never just "God and me" but always "God and we," which also includes the people who belong to the local Church I join. The possibility of multiple Higher Powers in our recoveries promises much more support—which is so vital!

We need visible Higher Powers that support us as we seek to discern where our life is taking and leading us. This underscores the value and importance of engaging with others, connecting not only with others in our recovery journeys but also connecting with and engaging with our Higher Powers—however many they may be.

I engage my Higher Powers by attending SAA meetings, meeting with my sponsor, meditating, being part of a local Catholic Church, and more.

The time has come to bring our Higher Powers out into the light and discover and recognize them in all parts of our lives. Keep this in mind as we explore these two Steps and the other Steps to come.

A KEY WORD IN STEP 2 IS SANITY

"Restore Us to Sanity"

Albert Einstein's definition of sanity is continuing to do the same thing over and over and expecting a different result.

Becoming sane is believing that through the help and support of my Higher Powers, I can change and do things differently. I don't have to stay in the same rut I have been in, for example, around my addictions. I can change with the help and support of others! For example, I can take a class and learn new ways of doing things, find a recovery group and continue to attend, exercise, etc. These are some ways to choose to develop new habits. This also involves making choices about what we *won't do* as well as what we *will do*.

Two other aspects of Step 2 relate directly to affirming the positive in our lives. The first is: as we seek to make changes and develop new habits, we must begin by taking slow and manageable steps. If we shoot too high, we will probably fail, which can only reinforce feeling that we are powerless. So start small and begin to build on successes, not failures.

That is seeking to build on positive successes.

The second affirmation of the positive is a willingness to be accountable for what we are trying to do. It is my experience that in being accountable to someone—a sponsor, a friend, a partner—is a game changer in seeking to become more sane.

We know that, as we seek to make changes in our lives, we will never do everything perfectly.

I love the line from *The Big Book* of AA in "How It Works": "It is about progress, not perfection."

If we can let go of trying to be perfect, we can AFFIRM the progress we are making with the help and support of others. It's really okay to be imperfect!

Why?

Because—truth be told—that is who we really are!

MOVING INTO STEP 3

Turn Over Our Wills and Lives to Our Higher Powers

Step 3 points to the importance of making decisions about the movement and desires of our lives in accord with what we value and who we want to be.

Our wills are the center of our ability to make decisions. For example, "I will . . . ."

Asking yourself, "Who do you want to be?" is a crucial part of Step 3. This process requires us to slow down in order to make choices about what is important "to me" rather than reactions that can trigger addictive behaviors.

Taking a deep breath, making a phone call, and taking a walk in nature are a few examples of ways to slow down in order to make choices that are in keeping with where we want our lives to go. We AFFIRM our ability to make choices with the help and support of others—our Higher Powers.

These two Steps invite us to continually AFFIRM our Higher Powers and give thanks to them. This helps us NURTURE greater HOPE.

Seeing that we can make choices and follow through on what we want to do helps us NURTURE greater HOPE for what we can do now and in the future.

REFLECTION QUESTIONS

1. Who/What are some of your Higher Powers? What makes someone or something a Higher Power for you?

2. What do you do when you feel like you are in the clutches of insanity?

3. Does making choices that lead to good results help you feel hopeful about your life?

CHAPTER IV

STEPS 4 & 5

STEP 4

Made a searching and **honest** inventory of ourselves.[3]

STEP 5

Admitted to a Higher Power, to ourselves, and to another human being the exact nature of our wrongs[4] **as well as the good things we have also done in our lives.**

Here again we are dealing with twin Steps. In Step 4, I have opted to replace **fearless** with **honest** in the wording of the Step—why? The usual word in this Step, "fearless," seems to imply a kind of perfectionism that can make the Step difficult

[3] Original wording has "fearless moral" inventory.

[4] Original wording ends after "our wrongs."

to do. Whenever I have done an inventory of my past, especially the first few times, I have felt some fear. I felt fear around looking back and seeing what I had done that hurt others and myself. I also feared what other actions I might discover that I did and had forgotten. That is why I think "honest" is a better word than "fearless" when it comes to making a searching self-inventory.

I also see the necessity and importance of courage in seeking to make an honest inventory of what we have done in our past. It takes courage to deal with our fears as we look back, as well as to look at any resentments we may still carry from things that were done to us in the past.

In looking back, it is also possible that we will remember experiences around which we still feel deep shame for whatever we did or didn't do. Looking back and doing a searching and honest inventory is very much like going swimming in the deep end of a pool—and knowing I am not a very good swimmer. One way to overcome this doubt or fear is to invite someone to go with us who can swim and will help us if we begin to drown.

Inviting a trusted person to come along with us as we do our inventory can help us keep some balance and help name things that we have done that caused harm. This could be a sponsor, a therapist, a spiritual director or a friend—just to name a few possibilities.

Doing an inventory can also lead us to feel as though we are truly drowning in shame. When that happens, it is good and beneficial to have a lifeguard along with us who can keep us from drowning.

In doing our inventory, we can also look at experiences where we continue to experience resentments about what happened to us and what other people might have done to us. We can remember experiences where we felt hopeless and frustrated by what happened and where these experiences led us.

As we look back, we may recognize the way in which we experienced traumas that may still have an impact upon our lives now. As I noted in the first chapter, all of us have experienced trauma to some degree in our lives, and these traumas continue to impact us and be part of our addictive behaviors. So again, we need safe places to begin to explore our traumas and having trusted people along is a necessary part of this. Processing past traumas is very difficult (if not impossible) to do alone. As I see it, asking for help is not a sign of weakness; rather, it is a sign of strength.

Whenever we are looking back and naming the wrongs we have done, we must also remember the good things we have done. Affirming the Positive all along the way in our recovery process is just as important as admitting our mistakes, *especially* as we are working on Steps 4 and 5. No one is all bad or has done only wrong things. We are each a composite of all we have done in life. That is the point in Erikson's Stages of Development where he describes the polarities at the different stages of our lives.

As we go through the different stages, our actions fall on both sides of the coin, such as experiences of intimacy as well as isolation. We need to name our actions on both sides of our lives—the wrongs we have done as well as the rights we have also done.

A trusted person can also be helpful here to remind us to look at both sides of our lives, especially when we get lost in shame for our misdeeds. In thinking about doing a personal inventory and sharing this with others, I remember the wisdom of Brené Brown, who has written much about shame and dealing creatively with shameful experiences.

She counsels that, when we begin to share experiences that are accompanied by shame, begin with a very small group of trusted people—not with the whole world. When you think of those you may want to share your Step 5 with, think about inviting a person or persons you trust, someone who will listen to you and not judge you.

Another possibility that emerges from looking back on our lives is a willingness to approach our past as a teacher might—a teacher like Jesus who has our best interests and our learning in mind. We can learn from our past—both what we did and didn't do.

Those learnings can help us live in the present as we look to our futures. In this way we AFFIRM our life and acknowledge the positives as well as the negatives.

This resonates and squares with the third promise of the 12 Promises of AA: "Do not regret the past nor wish to shut the door on it." As we AFFIRM our past, we are seeking to learn from our past and learning not to regret anything that happened or didn't happen. Being able to accomplish this is an enormous step toward accepting our lives and moving ahead with grace and confidence. This is also a way to generate HOPE for moving ahead in our lives. This can also lead us to experience and express gratitude for things in the past that possibly we only saw in a negative way.

Learning from our pasts can truly open us to giving thanks—always a good thing to do!

REFLECTION QUESTIONS

1. What part does fear play in your life? And what do you try to do with your fears?

2. Do you have trusted people in your life with whom you can share what you have done—the mistakes as well as the good things?

3. What is easier for you to share with others—the good things you have done, or the mistakes you have made, or possibly both?

CHAPTER V

STEPS 6 & 7

STEP 6

In completing the moral inventory of ourselves, we came to realize that we have behaviors that were and are harmful to others and ourselves.

Original STEP 6

Were entirely ready to have God remove all these defects of character.

In considering these twin Steps of 6 and 7, I must admit that I have struggled with these two Steps more than any others of the Twelve Steps.

Why?

I found myself reacting to the terms: "defects of character" and "shortcomings" that are used in the original wording of these steps.

STEP 7

Humbly asked **the help of our Higher Powers to gain the wisdom to know when to accept our limitations and imperfections and how to work at changing these behaviors.**

***Original* wording of STEP 7**

Humbly asked Him to remove our shortcomings.

When I hear those negative words, something inside of me recoils. I perceive them as an ideal trigger for feelings of shame. I hear this especially with the term "defects." To be defective is to be by one's very nature "less than." I hear the same in "shortcomings. Neither are "AFFIRMING" terms.

I take my reactions to these terms seriously because dealing with the shame we carry for what we did and/or didn't do because of our addictions is a challenge for all of us who struggle with addictions.

Once again, I appeal to the wisdom of Brené Brown, who talks about the difference between guilt and shame. I feel guilt when acknowledging my mistakes; I feel shame when I feel that I AM the mistake.

When I feel guilty, I can acknowledge my mistakes and make amends (more of this in Steps 8 and 9). Shame is much more of a feeling of drowning, disconnecting, and isolating. This can often lead us into further addictive behaviors in order to try to medicate the pain we are feeling in our shame.

At this point, I acknowledge again that my rewording of the Steps is tampering with wordings that have become enshrined and sacred to many, over many years. I realize that some people might take exception to or be disturbed by my rewording some Steps—such as Steps 6 and 7.

To some it may be akin to rewording the Ten Commandments! Some might even ask: "Who are you to go about doing this?"

My response is: I am trying to share what I have learned in working the Steps for almost thirty years, which, in this case, includes the genuine struggles I have had with some of the wording of some of the Steps. I also believe in the value of ongoing dialogue on issues that are important to me and us. To not engage in dialogue often leads to monologues and denial—neither of which are ever healthy.

I will cite as an example of denial the way the leaders of the Catholic Church chose to deal with the issue of pedophile priests. The leaders went into denial and continued that stance, and the abusive behavior continued until finally they were confronted with the evidence and forced to deal with the issue as well as all the pain associated with the abuse of so many for so long.

Being a member of a 12-Step group for almost thirty years has given me the opportunity to consider and suggest a few other ways of wording some of the Steps that will hopefully lead to more AFFIRMING of the positive messages as well as AFFIRMING HOPE in our recoveries.

What comes to me is the adage: Take what speaks to you and leave the rest.

In this vein, I chose **behaviors that were and are harmful to others and ourselves** (Step 6), and **limitations and imperfections** (Step 7). I also substituted **accept** for **remove** in Step 7.

I struggled as well with asking someone else—God or whomever else that person might be, to remove our shortcomings. I really see life as more of a collaborative venture between myself and others—even my Higher Powers. Looking to others to remove something feels like my being irresponsible. I can't just pass the ball to someone else and hope that they will take care of what is happening or not happening with me. I have to get involved in making the changes that I need to make with the help of others. I hear this as the essence of the words of the Serenity Prayer—asking for the wisdom to know when to accept what is, as well as the courage to make the changes we can.

One of my imperfections is my lack of patience. I can ask for the help and support of others to try to become more patient, and even be accountable to others for what I am trying do in becoming more patient. At the same time, I also need to do my part. That is, namely, practicing being patient and also acknowledging when I am not being patient.

Will I ever become a totally patient person? I doubt it. That doesn't stop me from trying to become more patient with the help of others. The lesson for me is that I need to do my part in making the changes I want to make.

A very important word in Step 7 is "humbly." As you know, I love to play with words and their roots. "Humbly" comes from a Latin word *humus*, meaning the earth, the soil. From this perspective, someone who is humble is one who is grounded in the earth and soil, like a tree. Because the tree is grounded, it can withstand storms and high winds. And we can learn from the trees who often live in forests with other trees who provide nourishment for each other.

Consider what might "humbly" might mean from this perspective. It is not being "humble" to put ourselves down or deny the gifts and talents we have been given. Instead, being humble means AFFIRMING who we are with our true gifts as well as our limitations—accepting the whole package that is each one of us.

Joining a 12-Step group is an exercise in humility—asking for and accepting the help and support of others in changing our addictive behaviors and realizing that we could not do this on our own and alone.

Acknowledging when we need to ask for help from others is a humble exercise that gives us HOPE to continue our work in recovery.

REFLECTION QUESTIONS

1. What does "humbly" mean to you? Do you see yourself as a humble person? How so?

2. Whom can you call upon to help and support you in the changes you want to make?

3. What behaviors at this point in your life cause harm to others and yourself?

CHAPTER VI

STEPS 8 & 9

STEP 8

Made a list of persons we have harmed and became willing to make amends to them all **as well as making a list of the people who have helped and supported us.**[5]

STEP 9

Made direct amends to the people we have harmed, wherever possible, except when to do so would injure them, others**, or ourselves, and to reach out and give thanks to the people who have helped and supported us.**[6]

[5] The original Step 8 ends at "them all."

[6] The original Step 9 ends after "others."

My rewording of these twin Steps 8 and 9 arises from a conversation I recently had with a fellow I have sponsored for a number of years. Bill, the gentleman's name, shared with me an experience he had while attending the funeral service of a very important person in his life, someone who had helped him to take a deeper look into his spirituality.

Bill spoke about how important it was for him to attend the funeral and join with many others in celebrating this person's life. Being present there generated deep thankfulness in Bill for what this person had given him.

As he shared this story with me, and as I was working on these Steps for this book, I had the awareness these two Steps needed more—not only listing and reaching out to others we had harmed, but also reaching out and thanking the people who helped us along the way.

Once again, this is adding space in these Steps for AFFIRMING the POSITIVES—in this case, people who have helped us by walking with us, those who did not walk away from us. This is a source of HOPE for us as we struggle with our addictions and recoveries.

Another dimension I added is to include ourselves as someone we also need to make amends to for what we have done to hurt ourselves with our addictive behaviors. At the same time, we must give ourselves thanks for the good things that we also have been able to do to help ourselves and others—such as joining 12-Step groups to confront and recover from our addictions. We need to make amends as well as give thanks to ourselves.

At the heart of Step 8 is the word "willingness"—a willingness to make a list of people we have harmed. And here I included listing those also who have helped us. I recognize the wisdom in separating these (as these Steps do) with making the lists and actually reaching out. In working Step 8, please don't forget to include yourself as someone you harmed. Step 8 as preparing us for the further work—a warm-up for more challenging work that we do in Step 9. This is like spring training for baseball teams as they prepare for the full season ahead.

In approaching Step 9, I urge caution in reaching out to others to make direct amends for what we have done to harm them. And that, as we consider making direct amends to others, another person to keep in mind is ourselves. We do not want to cause more harm for ourselves as we think about making direct amends to another. Self-care is a value I have come to prize in working the Twelve Steps. Bottom line, we often forget ourselves in working the Steps.

Please, remember YOURSELF! You are very important and deserving of care, forgiveness, and love.

With regard to these two Steps, I raise something again that is very helpful—if not extremely crucial: have a trusted person to walk and talk with when thinking about those we will make direct amends to. Shame and guilt can complicate this process of making direct amends, and it can be extremely helpful to have someone to talk to about the next steps we are considering.

It is not nurturing yourself to walk alone and try to figure out everything on your own. We do not want to injure ourselves any more than we already have, nor do we need to open a pandora's box that has been hopefully closed for a time. Especially here, it is important to have a trusted person to walk with us.

I will share a few experiences I have had in working these two Steps. When I was rather new to the program and working Step 9, I was aware of a person I had harmed. I was also aware that there had been some legal issues involved in the situation that prevented me from approaching this person.

I raised my concerns with the group, and one of the more veteran members said that one of the ways to make amends when a direct amend is not possible is to work our program of recovery and commit to not harming others. I have never forgotten his wisdom and have shared his wisdom with many others. Our commitment to working the Steps as an option when direct amends are not possible is a way to deal with feeling powerless. This suggestion gave me a perspective that also gave me HOPE in making direct amends, which can be frightening.

I have made direct amends to others I had harmed and received different types of responses. The first was a "thank you" for my making a direct amend to the person. Another person said something like there was "no need to make the amend" to them, as they felt they were equally involved in the harm. I share these stories to say that this process of making direct amends is always filled with many unknowns and different reactions. It can be risky to do this process on one's own. Walking and talking with a trusted person about what to do, as well as processing what happened when making a direct amend, is wise self-care.

In this regard, I love the song, "Lean on Me."

I am a firm believer in the value of saying thanks and expressing gratitude to others who have helped and supported us over the years, especially as we struggled with our addictions and moved into recovery. I often remember the words of the Creator at the beginning of the Hebrew Bible in the Book of Genesis: “It is not good for the man to be alone. I will make him a helper as his partner” (Genesis 2:18).

Yes, it is not good for us humans to be alone! We need help and partners on our recovery journeys, especially in a Step, like Step 9, which can be complicated. I don’t think we can profess enough thanks to those people who have walked with us and continue to partner with us.

This particular issue is so important to me that I wrote my book about gratitude, in which I added the important concept of gratitude to the Serenity Prayer. Basically, when we ask and we receive, it is always good to give thanks to others and also to ourselves.

The world yearns for more gratitude. And it is difficult to feel resentment when we are feeling grateful!

REFLECTION QUESTIONS

1. Have people ever made amends to you about what they did to harm you? How did you respond?

2. Who are some of the people you have harmed and have you made any kind of direct amends to them? Why yes or why not?

3. Who are some of the people you want to express your gratitude to for the ways they have stuck with you and supported you over the years?

CHAPTER VII

STEP 10

STEP 10

We continue to take personal inventory and admit
to ourselves and others in a timely fashion
when we were wrong as well as when we were right.

The original wording of Step 10 was shorter:

Original **STEP 10**

Continued to take personal inventory and
when we were wrong promptly admitted it.

If you have followed my thinking so far, my addition to this Step will come as no surprise.

Here I continue to inject and AFFIRM the POSITIVE in seeking to balance the wrongs and the rights we have done. It is unhealthy to only acknowledge the wrongs we have done. We need to acknowledge both sides of the coin of behaviors and actions in our lives—just as Erickson lists both sides of the coin in each of his Stages of Development. Both extremes acknowledge the struggles we go through in developing as people from infancy to old age.

Neither side is a simple walk in the park!

I have often found myself struggling with the original word "promptly." For me, this word again seems to suggest an expectation of perfectionism—suggesting that we must be aware of and make all our admissions "right away."

Instead, I suggest admitting what we have done wrong in "a reasonable amount of time." And this starts our willingness to first recognize and admit to ourselves that what we did was wrong. Many of us find it difficult to admit a wrong to another—especially if we are still in denial about our wrongdoing.

I have noticed a shift in the last three of the Twelve Steps, as they seem to call us to be more aware of what is taking place in our lives *here and now*. Much has been written about the importance of living in present—in the now. The past is past and, though we can learn from the past, we will not be healthy if we live in the past. That is the stuff of nostalgia (the good old days) or perhaps beating up ourselves for what we did or didn't do back then.

The future is not here yet. What we have is the present!

Truly seeking to live in present time—the Now—is the focus of Steps 10, 11 and 12.

Some areas to reflect upon as we continue to do a personal inventory in present time include asking ourselves:

Do I feel hopeless about my life or in situations where I find myself?

What or who scares and frightens me these days?

What is causing my frustrations?

Did I show courage in any situation recently?

Did I engage with others in healthy ways?

Was I able to express my creativity in any way?

Was I aware of Higher Powers at work in my life?

These questions are examples of what I raised by looking at both sides of my own life—acknowledging potential mistakes as well as the positive and creative things I did.

I applied this approach to try to AFFIRM the positives as well as NURTURE HOPE—my focus in this book.

We must keep our practices manageable to assure the most positive and successful results. If we try to do too much, or if what we are trying to do becomes unmanageable, we will find ourselves back to Step 1—feeling powerless and possibly feeling like a failure, which can lead us back into addictive behaviors.

For example, if we try to begin meditating every day for fifteen minutes and find we are not able to do that daily—try a different approach to the goal—as promoted in *The Big Book of AA*—strive for progress, not perfection. This is extremely important to keep in mind in relation to any of the practices we choose to help us in our sobriety and self-care.

Another suggestion is to reexamine and perhaps redefine the words we are using. For example, the word "daily" usually means twenty-four hours of time.

But there may be too much to do in our lives to fit in every single need or expectation: work, family involvements, recovery practices, meetings, etc.

So why not give a new meaning to "daily?" The most significant meaning in the word is consistency or regularity, not necessarily the twenty-four hours that make up a day.

How about an intention like this instead?

We will do all that we need to and want to do in forty-eight hours (or try your own idea of a reasonable time period for completion).

The key is to help set ourselves up for success.

Examining our language and redefining terms can help us put progress ahead of perfection and allow us to accomplish what we want to do in order to remain healthy and sober.

Isn't progress the goal of our recovery practices?

REFLECTION QUESTIONS

1. What helps you progress in your life these days?

2. How easy or difficult is it these days for you to live in present time?

3. Do you do any kind of regular inventory about what is going on in your life? If so, how do you do this?

CHAPTER VIII

STEP 11

Original STEP 11

Sought through prayer and meditation to improve our contact with **God, praying only for knowledge of His will for us** and the power to **carry that out**.

Step 11 is a tricky Step, as we are confronted again with practices like prayer and meditation and the use of "God" language in the original wording. Again I use Higher Powers in my revised version of Step 11:

STEP 11

Sought thorough prayer and meditation to improve our **conscious contact with our Higher Powers,** praying only for **a clearer awareness of who we are called to be,** and the power to **become that person.**

An ongoing discussion about whether the Twelve Steps are more like a religion is seen in a more recent phenomenon that refers to people called "Nones." A number of studies have been conducted and books have been written about the increasing number of folks (Nones) who have disconnected from attending any churches or being part of any religious traditions.

And the numbers only seem to keep growing.

In his book, *The Nones*, Ryan Burge estimates that about 30 percent of the US population are Nones. More and more people are deciding to abandon participation in churches. This is important because churches—for good or for ill—have been influential for people finding supportive communities to which to belong as well as supporting the learning and living of values and beliefs.

Back to the Surgeon General's Report mentioned earlier: one out of every two Americans are experiencing loneliness and disconnection in their lives.

I think we are at a crisis point as a country in terms of our well-being. Loneliness and disconnection are very often a heavy-traveled road into addiction. With organized religion and church communities becoming less important in peoples' lives, where can we go to find community?

My own participation in the SAA group I have attended for almost thirty years has provided me with a spiritual framework that has helped me find recovery. I also experience community at the Catholic Church my wife and I attend, which is very supportive of both of us.

I will take some space here to share my journey to spirituality as being a very important component of how I view religion in positive ways even if I can also agree it is not perfect:

The person who helped me clarify the difference between a strictly religious program and one that was open to a person's "spirituality" was the person who taught me journaling—Dr. Ira Progoff. This Jewish psychologist created a method of journaling called the Intensive Journal as described in his book *At a Journal Workshop: Writing to Access the Power of Unconscious and Evoke Creative Ability*. The workshops he taught on his method drew many Catholic people, especially religious women and priests in the 1960s and 1970s. Gratefully, I was one of them. Dr. Progoff's journaling method took an interesting turn in 1980 when he wrote, *The Practice of Process Meditation: The Intensive Journal Way to Spiritual Experience*. He added five sections to the original Journal, dealing with spiritual experiences.

Earlier, he had written a book on a spiritual classic called *The Cloud of Unknowing*, which included his translation of this classic. My sense is that Dr. Progoff continued to struggle to present a way to view spirituality that would make sense to modern people and point out how spirituality is a very important part of every person's life—not just people who go to a church or a synagogue or a mosque!

He saw spirituality as a faculty within each of us—like our memories and imaginations—whose function was to help us find meaning and purpose in our lives. Spirituality is about meaning and purpose. He also defined spiritual experiences as those of connection and disconnection that impact the meaning of our lives. Our journeys to meaning might involve belonging to churches or synagogues or mosques, or it might not.

Another part of Ira Progoff's life is related to his own life story. He wrote his doctoral dissertation on Carl Jung's "Social Meaning." What Ira told us in the workshops I attended was that Jung was so surprised that he had a "social meaning," he wanted to meet the guy who discovered this. So Jung invited Ira to come to Zurich and study with him. Ira accepted Jung's invitation.

As this interesting time in Jung's life was nearing an end, he was deeply seeking to understand the concept of synchronicity. For Jung, synchronicity was another principle at work in the universe besides cause-and-effect. He thought of synchronicity as those experiences that we might label "chance" or "accident."

Jung's study impacted Ira, who wrote a book on the topic, as did Jung. Studying with Progoff also influenced me regarding the importance of synchronicity and my deeper understanding of spirituality. My experiences of synchronicity often come as I look back and remember things in life that have happened. Remembering is an important part of discovering or recognizing the synchronistic.

Before suggesting further practices for Step 11, I will address the meaning of this Step, which has many moving parts. Basically, Step 11 focuses on the importance of seeking to be conscious in our lives and in our recoveries. That is the opposite of reacting to triggers. It is about making choices concerning what we want to do.

This Step points to developing practices of prayer and meditation that help us to stay conscious and awake through connection with our Higher Powers. And this involves finding ways—prayer and meditation—that allow us to speak as well as listen to our Higher Powers and help us become more aware of who we are called to be, and to find the strength and energy to become that person.

Now to consider some practices of prayer and meditation.

JOURNALING

After detailing how significant Ira Progoff has been and continues to be in my life, it is probably no surprise that the first practice I suggest and strongly endorse is journaling. Clearly, journaling is not for everyone. But for many, journaling is a good way to keep track of what is going on in one's life as well as being able to look back on what on our life has taught us and is still teaching us.

At the heart of journaling in my experience is the opportunity and ability to write for my own eyes alone. Journaling provides a space to say what is going on without fearing judgments or criticisms from anyone else. We can, if we wish, share what we write and, again, only to people we trust.

A couple of journaling prompts to start writing:

What was yesterday like? What happened?

What feelings and thoughts were you aware of?

Take a memory—let any memory come to you—and write about what took place. Then carry your learning from that experience to help you with whatever is going on in your life right now.

Describe how you feel right now.

Any prompt that gets us writing is a plus. Go with what comes to you as you write.

MINDFULNESS

A term for meditation that has become popular is called mindfulness. This involves becoming aware of oneself and one's breathing. This means taking the time to stop, find a comfortable place, and follow the rhythm of our breathing—in and out slowly. With this practice, we slow down and calm ourselves. This is especially helpful in trying to balance the hectic lives many of us live.

To embark on developing this practice, begin with short periods of time focused on breathing and gradually expand the length as you become more accustomed to this practice. As a reminder, we need to keep our practices manageable so that we don't fall back into Step 1 and feel powerless.

Our meditation practices need to be manageable. We are not a failure if our meditation practice is short. Even five or ten minutes can be effective. Quality of practice is more important than the quantity of time spent meditating. Even expanding the time in meditation for one moment is one more success.

THE SERENITY PRAYER AND GRATITUDE

The Serenity Prayer

God grant me the serenity to accept
the things I cannot change,
The courage to change the things I can,
And the wisdom to know the difference.

Though the practice of praying may not appeal to some or many may not feel comfortable, let me explain an experience

I had when I first joined my SAA group. The meeting began and ended with the Serenity Prayer, which is a common practice for many 12-Step groups.

I felt comfortable and at one with the sentiments of this prayer. I fell so in love with this prayer that I began to say it at other times than just at the meetings.

As I said the Serenity Prayer, I became aware that each line was a request—for serenity, courage, and wisdom. In my Catholic tradition of prayer, one of the ways to pray is to request what we need and want; another is to give thanks for what we have already been given.

That awareness led me to add another sentiment to this prayer—Gratitude:

> I am grateful for the serenity, courage,
> and wisdom you have given me.

I even wrote a book on the topic: *The Gratitude Element: A New Look at the Serenity Prayer*. In doing the research for that book, I found much that confirmed that developing a regular practice of giving thanks leads to a healthier life—physically, emotionally, and psychologically. That is also why I added the Stage of Gratitude vs. Gratefulness to Erickson's Stages of Development. Expressing gratitude can be a game-changer in living healthy lives and living in sobriety.

One way of praying is asking our Higher Powers for what we need—such as the courage to do something we may feel is hard to do. This could include asking a person for the support to do this difficult thing or being accountable for trying to do the difficult thing. Praying is inviting our Higher Powers to walk with us and help us—we don't have to do the hard stuff alone!

You can use the Serenity Prayer as a model of praying if you are looking for ways to pray and may feel unsure about how to pray, or even if you might feel uncomfortable praying.

Use what someone else created to help you!

AFFIRMATIONS

Another way to pray and meditate is with affirmations—repeating positive messages. The use of affirmations is a powerful way to counter negative self-talk.

Some examples of affirmations to be said as often as desired are:

"I am okay!"

"I am creative and resourceful!"

"I am loveable!"

"I am hopeful!"

These are really simple expressions that AFFIRM the person saying them—another way to AFFIRM the POSITIVE!

This practice helps to challenge negative thoughts that come to mind when we are struggling or have made a mistake. Affirmations help us move out of Step 1—powerlessness—by changing what we are saying to ourselves and about ourselves.

Try it, it might be a helpful way for you.

LIFE PURPOSE STATEMENT

One of the many, many great ways to practice prayer and meditation is with what I call a Life Purpose Statement. I have found that creating such a statement is helpful as a way to focus on what and who we are trying to be, and what we want to do in this present time of our lives.

A reminder of our Life Purpose can be especially helpful when we are feeling lost, adrift, and powerless. Such a statement doesn't have to be long—rather, it is a short statement that gives expression to what we value and believe.

Journaling can help here. Begin to write down some of the values you hold to be important. Some of mine are: respect of others, finding supportive communities, self-care, gratitude, and resilience. From these values, you can create a Life Purpose Statement. I once crafted the following statement:

"I want to belong to communities where
we help and support each other to be able to rebound
from adversities and challenges."

Such statements help us focus, especially when we feel out of focus. We can return and reread what we wrote to help us refocus. Also, such statements are not necessarily forever—here and now they express what is important to us to help stay on the path of recovery and creativity.

Incidentally, I prefer the term creativity to generativity in Erickson's Stages, because we are all called to give expression—to be creative in deciding what is important to us and what we value most in life.

This is important in our recoveries and can serve well as an opening for us to NURTURE our HOPE.

COMMUNITY PRAYER AND MEDITATION

In addition to the importance of practicing ways of remaining conscious is gathering with others to pray and meditate. Without stretching this too far, a 12-Step meeting is an effective way a group gathers to practice Step 11 with readings, the Serenity Prayer, and speaking and listening to one another.

I have found that when a group gathers to pray—a Church service with good music and reflections, a group journaling together (as I learned from Progoff), and a conversation with a good friend that touches on what is important to each of the people are a few examples of the power that can tapped when people gather to pray and meditate together.

Again, this brings to the fore the importance of communities in our lives and in our recoveries. They help us AFFIRM the POSITIVES as well as NURTURE HOPE.

Remember, there are many, many ways to pray and meditate. I have listed a few that have been helpful to me. As Step 11 suggests, remaining conscious and in contact with our Higher Powers help us to stay on track with what is important in our lives and these include different ways of speaking and listening to our Higher Powers and to one another.

REFLECTION QUESTIONS

1. How do you seek to remain conscious in your life?

2. Do you have ways to pray and meditate? If you do, what are some of your favorites?

3. Which of your Higher Powers do you connect with most frequently? How do you do this?

CHAPTER IX

STEP 12

STEP 12

Having had a spiritual **awakening** as a result of **these Steps**, we tried to carry this message to **all others who are part of our lives** and to practice these principles in all our affairs.

We have reached Step 12, the culmination of working the prior Steps of 1 through 11. From my experiences, there are two ways to work the Steps. The first is simply moving through the Steps from 1 to 12.

An abundance of insights come in working the Steps in such an orderly fashion. I also sense a creative energy that arises when we work the Steps in this kind of orderly progression.

Another way happens, however, in the day-to-day as we live our lives—when events happen that thrust us back into Step 1, feeling powerless and searching for Higher Powers to support and help us.

Both ways are part of our recovery journeys, so don't be surprised when life throws you a curve ball and you bounce from Step 10 to Step 1, for example. That is the nature of life and the nature of recovery and working the Steps—sometimes orderly and sometimes out of order. That's life, and that's recovery!

Step 12 begins with speaking about having had a spiritual "awakening" as a result of working these Steps. What then is a spiritual awakening? In a way, this means different things to different people—as is true of many terms used in the Twelve Steps. In studying the literature related to this, it seems to mean that a change—an awakening—came about that led us to change our perceptions and our behaviors. For example, the changes that led us to move from a life impacted by addictions to a way of life that more embodies recovery practices.

I recall the key axiom—progress, not perfection. A spiritual awakening is not becoming perfect; it is much more about making progress in our recovery program.

Awakenings can come in different ways. I suggest that some are directly related to working the Steps, while others may not seem to be.

An awakening example from my own life was realizing that I was addicted, which then led me to search for and find an SAA group. In looking back, I also believe there was a synchronicity that led me to this group where I have found a true home.

Awakenings can also come when someone gives us feedback about something we were blind to, which brings about an awakening or realization that leads to change. Awakenings can come as we work a program like the Twelve Steps that leads us into looking at aspects of our life that we had buried or hadn't looked at for a long time.

An awakening, whatever be the causes, gives us the possibility of seeing things differently in our lives that then lead to different ways of acting. We can see behaviors that hurt others, and we can commit to changing. Or we can discover times when we were there for others and really helped them, and AFFIRM the POSITIVE we have done.

Awakenings can be about almost any dimension of our lives and, at times, they can be surprising about what they reveal about our lives—things we didn't always see. These events wake us up and often face us with new choices!

Step 12 raises the challenge of carrying the message and principles to others. The outreach spoken of here is more than just with the addicts we are connected with. For me, this has come to mean carrying the message and practicing the principles with everyone we meet—not with just a few folks. Step 12 reminds us that the purpose of all the Steps is more than just stopping addictive behaviors.

I understand Step 12 as a culmination of working all the Steps and being of service to others—as the Step states: "in all of our affairs." This is continually asking, "Where can I be of service to others?"

I was recently struck by a book I read about male depression, *I Don't Want to Talk about It: Overcoming the Secret Legacy of Male Depression* by Terrence Real, who discusses and exposes the heavy burden we men often carry as a result of difficult experiences with our dads. These often lead us to carry depression from generation to generation. What I found most interesting was a suggestion that he makes toward the end of the book, which I see as being much in step with Step 12.

He describes an essential shift in a question we ask ourselves that is necessary in transforming a depressed man. A shift from "*What will I get?*" to "*What can I offer?*" hits at the heart of Step 12, and this is a willingness to look out of ourselves to see how we might be of service to others—or what can we offer to others?

The motto of the St Joan of Arc Catholic Church in Minneapolis that my wife and I belong to is: "We welcome you wherever you are on your journey."

This sentiment is another way of challenging ourselves to extend beyond ourselves in service to others and practice these principles in our lives—noted in each of the Twelve Steps:

Step 1. *Honesty* in acknowledging where we are powerless and struggling

Step 2. *Community* in acknowledging Higher Powers

Step 3. *Surrender* to Higher Powers

Step 4. *Courage* to look into our lives and do a searching inventory

Step 5. *Openness* to share our inventory with others

Step 6. *Willingness* to admit our gifts and our imperfections

Step 7. *Humility* to ask for help

Step 8. *Developing awareness* of whom we hurt and whom has helped us

Step 9. Seek *forgiveness* and make amends as well as giving thanks

Step 10. *Reflection*

Step 11. *Consciousness awareness*

Step 12. *Service*

Some of Erickson's Stages of Development are principles as well—such as hope or integrity, intimacy, creativity, generativity and industry. These principles came clear to me as I looked over the Steps. I know others have shared other principles, and you may have done the same.

What is important to remember is that the Steps are not just for reflection. They are for ACTION! The Twelve Steps call us to come out of isolation and find the "WEs" that can support and challenge us to not only continue to choose sobriety but also to be of service to others.

Another aspect of recovery deals with falling back and relapsing into addictive behaviors, especially when we might have remained sober for a good long time. This might sound heretical—but I see slips are part of recovery.

My own experience and that of others says to me that events happen in our lives that trigger us back into addictive behaviors. We walk past a bar, the smells draw us in, and we begin to drink; we click on a website and all of a sudden we are looking at porn; our codependency is triggered when we see someone in trouble and can't back away—to name a few examples.

Such moments present us with a choice—we can bury ourselves in shame and isolate, or we can reach out, check in, and recommit to our recovery practices. Bottom line, all of us—including myself—are imperfect people who need the WEs of our life to be supported *and* to support others.

Bottom line: Recovery is a two-way street!

Beware then of one-way streets!

REFLECTION QUESTIONS

1. What do you make of spiritual awakenings? Have you ever had one?

2. How do you try to be service to others these days? Do you let others be of service to you?

3. How do you view slips in your recovery program? What do you do after a slip?

Chapter X

Epilogue

I end with a series of awarenesses that have emerged in my writing that complement the focus of this book on how to AFFIRM the positive and NURTURE hope as we looked at the Twelve Steps and provide some alternative wording to some of the Steps.

THE STORY OF THE PRODIGAL SON

This is a parable that Jesus told in Luke's Gospel in Chapter 15:11–32. I have chosen to tell the story rather than quote it. This message about a father and his sons could also apply to daughters and a mother.

The younger son of a man with two sons asked his father for his share of his inheritance, which the father gives him.

The son went off and squandered all that he had been given and eventually finds himself working as a hired hand. He realizes that he could return home and work for his father and be in a better place. As he nears home, his father sees him coming and runs out to greet his son and warmly welcomes him home. The son (possibly because of the embarrassment of realizing what he had done in squandering his inheritance) says he is only interested in working for his father. But the father will not hear of this and declares it was time for a celebration to welcome his son home—the son who was lost, has returned home.

The older son hears the sounds of celebration as he comes closer and asks about the reason for the celebration. When he learns that his brother has returned and that is the reason for celebration, he goes to his father and expresses his displeasure. He says he has been obedient and always done what was expected of him, and his father has never thrown a party for him.

The father explains that there is a reason to celebrate—the son who was lost has come home. The older brother chooses to have no part in the celebration of his brother's return home.

What triggered such a response from the older brother? How often can the feeling that we are overlooked or not seen lead us to get angry and upset? Such feelings can often lead us into a negative perspective on life.

In this parable, however, the father chose to AFFIRM the POSITIVE in welcoming home the younger son, even though he had squandered all of his inheritance. The father also conveyed HOPE to the younger son by welcoming him home.

To AFFIRM the POSITIVE is a choice we have to make time after time as we have different life experiences. We need people—like the loving parent—to welcome us back when we have made mistakes or lost our way.

The added challenge for us is to welcome back other people we know and meet, choosing to AFFIRM the POSITIVE, and not to be sidetracked by the negatives and mistakes. Give others HOPE for their futures too.

SELF-CARE

Self-Care is an essential element of recovery and working the Twelve Steps. Care of our bodies is an important part of our recovery. Recovery is more than just a mind trip! Recovery entails nurturing our bodies by committing to practices such as exercise and movement, good sleep, and a healthy diet.

What this looks like for each person will differ. Taking care of our health, as a critical part of our commitment to recovery, is part of affirming the positives of our bodies. Many women and men have learned and embedded deep shame about our bodies from messages from others as well as the messages that come from society and the media about what an attractive, svelte body should look like.

All bodies are probably less than perfect, and we need to support and own our bodies *as they are* as we commit to self-care. Consulting with clinicians and other professionals about tending to our bodies and our self-care is another dimension of Steps 2 and 3. They can be Higher Powers who help us.

An example from my own life emerged a number of years ago when my wife told me that I sometimes stopped breathing during the night. I mentioned this to my doctor who recommended a sleep study.

The study discovered that I was awakening many times each night. Those kinds of awakenings were not healthy. I was prescribed and have been using a CPAP machine to assist with my sleeping, which has made a difference in the quality of my life and our lives.

Another example of self-care is that my wife and I do Pilates together once a week. Our bodies do not belong in a separate compartment from the Twelve Steps and/or our recovery programs. To neglect our bodies puts added stress on our recoveries and can become triggers for further addictive behaviors.

RITUALS

The last topic I want to stress in concluding this book is the importance of rituals in our daily lives. On one hand, some rituals have been part of our addictive practices—going to a particular place, performing the same behaviors each time, spending time with the same people, walking down the same street, to name a few. Rituals can often be habits that we have developed as part of our addictions, and trying to change these rituals and habits can often make recovery very challenging.

I have found it helpful to replace addictive rituals with recovery rituals. I have a morning ritual—get up, shower, eat breakfast, meditate, and journal. I perform this morning ritual on most days, and this gets my days off to a good start.

Attending my weekly SAA meeting is another recovery ritual. Since I attend on most Wednesday evenings, I don't have to think about what I will do on Wednesday evenings. While there, I also learn more about the Twelve Steps as we share our experiences around the Steps during the last week. I also share coffee with a group three mornings each week.

I attend Church services most Sunday mornings. These and other rituals help me stay focused as well as allow me to celebrate important events in the lives of other people who make up the groups that are important to me.

Self-care (especially of our bodies) and developing nurturing rituals are important adjuncts to working the Twelve Steps. In my experience, they really do facilitate the working of the Steps and keep us aware that our bodies are an essential component of our recoveries.

Recovery doesn't just happen when we think about it. We have to get off the couch and move and act!

As you work the Twelve Steps, please always remember that perfection doesn't exist in this world—we all make mistakes. With this in mind, I suggest two songs to listen to as we walk into recovery: "We Are Not Alone" and "Lean on Me." Both songs speak of the value and importance of community and support in our journeys.

Lastly and most importantly, don't forget to AFFIRM the POSITIVE—both in yourself and in others—which is a valuable way to NURTURE HOPE. Each help us find a way to return home when we have lost our way or have lost confidence in ourselves.

As you walk the Twelve Steps of Recovery, remember to find ways to AFFIRM the POSITIVE in others as well as yourself, which gives reasons to have HOPE, even when life is challenging.

Though there are twelve, remember to take ONE STEP AT A TIME!

Thank you for walking up and down these Steps with me!

ANNOTATED BIBLIOGRAPHY SUGGESTED READING

Arlen, H. and J. Mercer. *Accentuate the Positive.* Music by Harold Arlen and lyrics by Johnny Mercer, 1944.

Brown, Brené. *Daring Greatly: How the Courage to be Vulnerable Transforms the Way We Love, Parent, and Lead.* USA: Penguin Putnam, Inc., 2017. [An important contribution to helping us move out of the shame often associated with addictive behaviors and move into recovery.]

Burge, Ryan, *The Nones: Where They Came From, Who They Are and Where They Are Going.* Minneapolis: Fortress Press, 2nd Edition, 2023. [Describes the research as well as the future ramifications of people no longer attending and being members of churches.]

Chestnut, Glenn F. *Father Ed Dowling: Bill Wison's Sponsor.* Bloomington, IN, iUniverse, 2015. [Fascinating book about the beginnings of AA from the perspective of a Catholic priest and mentor to Bill W, the founder of AA.]

DeVito, Karla. *We Are Not Alone.* Lyrics by Karle DeVito, 1985.

Frankl, Viktor. *Man's Search for Meaning: An Introduction to Logotherapy.* Boston, MA: Beacon Press, 2006.

Holy Bible, New Revised Standard Version. Catholic Bible Press: Nashville Thomas Nelson, Inc., 1993.

Howe, Reuel L. *The Miracle of Dialogue.* New York: Seabury Press, 1963. [Seminal book on moving from monologue into dialogue, and the miracles that take place.]

Jung, Carl. "Synchronicity: An Acausal Connective Principle" from *Collective Works of C. G. Jung, Vol 8*, New York: Pantheon Books, 1960. [Seminal work that opens the topic of synchronicity, what it means and how it is experienced.]

Kurtz, Ernie. *Not God: A History of Alcoholics Anonymous.* Center City, MN: Hazelden, 1991. [This book opened up for me the possibility of looking at synchronicity more inclusively and provides ways to dialogue about this in relation to the Twelve Steps.]

Magness, Steve and Brad Stulberg. *Peak Performance.* NY, NY: Rodale Books, 2017. [This book touches on important issues of living in recovery: managing stress, finding ways to rest, and living with purpose.]

Marich, Jamie. *Trauma and the 12 Steps.* Berkeley, California: North Atlantic Books, 2020. [Sensitive treatment of how 12-Step groups can better respond to struggles with traumas.]

Murthy, MD, MBA, Vivek. *Our Epidemic of Loneliness and Isolation: The U.S. Surgeon General's Advisory on the Healing Effects of Social Connection and Community.* May 2023.

Progoff, Ira. *Jung, Synchronicity, and Human Destiny: C. G. Jung's Theory of Meaningful Coincidence.* New York: Julian Press, 1973. [Personal story of the first meeting between Jung and Progoff that launched Progoff's exposure to synchronicity.]

Progoff, Ira. *At a Journal Workshop: Writing to Access the Power of the Unconscious and Evoke Creative Ability.* New York: Dialogue House Library, 1975. [The basic resource book on the Intensive Journal method.]

Progoff, Ira. *The Practice of Process Meditation: The Intensive Journal Way to Spiritual Experience.* New York: Dialogue House Library, 1980. [This journaling method helps people discover and work with their spiritual experiences to make sense out of them.]

Progoff, Ira. *A New* Translation *of the Classic 14th-Century Guide to Spiritual Experience.* New York: Delta Books, 1989. [Foundational work for Progoff's later work using a spiritual classic to develop his ideas about spirituality.]

Real, Terrence. *I Don't Want to Talk about IT: Overcoming the Secret Legacy of Male Depression.* New York: Scribner, 1997. [Powerful book not only in dealing with male depression and its causes, it also contains many stories of his clients and himself in seeking to deal with male depression. He also references the relationship between male depression and addictions. In this regard, he shares his beliefs about how important recovery groups are in helping a person deal with his depression.]

Scannell, Mark T. *The Gratitude Element: A New Look at the Serenity Prayer.* Minneapolis, MN: Gasscann Publishers, 2015. [Gratitude emerges as an important addition to the time-honored Serenity Prayer.]

Scannell, Mark T. *Resilience: The Ability to Rebound from Adversity.* Minneapolis, MN: Gasscann Publishers, 2019. [How to develop a much-needed quality for life.]

Scannell, Mark T. *The Village It Takes: The Power to Affirm.* Minneapolis, MN: Gasscann Publishers, 2021. [This book stresses the importance of finding communities/villages to support and affirm us in our lives.]

Schaef, Ann Wilson. *When Society Becomes an Addict.* San Francisco, California: Harper One Publishers, 1988. [Important book suggesting that not only individuals are addicted, but groups as well, which impacts the individuals in groups as well as their recoveries.]

Van Der Kolk, MD, Bessel. *The Body Keeps the Score.* New York: Penguin Books, 2014. [Eloquent account of the impact of traumas and how to heal from traumas.]

Wilson, Bill W. *The Big Book of Alcoholics Anonymous.* New York: AA World Services, 1939. [The foundations of AA provide perspective on its origins and influences.]

Withers, Bill. *Lean on Me:* Lyrics by Bill Withers. 1972.

ACKNOWLEDGMENTS

I have learned that none of us is an island, and we are continually drawing upon the connections we have with others in living our lives as well as undertaking any large project, such as writing a book.

I especially thank two people who have been instrumental in creating this book. I thank Marly Cornell for her help editing the manuscript into its finished form and offering much good feedback. I also thank long-time friend and colleague, Marie Thielen, for her photo of steps for the book cover. The Steps come alive in seeing actual steps.

I also acknowledge the many people whose wisdom and experiences I have drawn upon in writing this book. Some of their works are included in the Bibliography; others have arisen out of personal contacts over the years.

I close with a final gratitude thought from my last book about the importance of villages. We need villages to live day by day, in order to create, to rejoice, and to cry. No one of us is an island! And I am grateful for that every day!

ABOUT THE AUTHOR

Originally from the Chicago suburb of Oak Park, Illinois, Mark attended Catholic schools through high school. He attended the University of Notre Dame for two years and, in 1962, he joined a Catholic religious community of priests and brothers, called the Dominican Order.

Mark was ordained a priest in 1969 amid all the changes taking place in the Catholic Church after the Second Vatican Council. In preparing for ordination, he studied philosophy and theology, earning Master's degrees in both.

A significant moment took place in the early 1970s when he met psychologist Ira Progoff, the creator of the Intensive Journal method and other works related to spirituality. While leading journaling workshops around the country, Dr. Progoff became a mentor for Mark, who then became a leader of the workshops and presented them around the US for many years.

Mark left the priesthood and the religious community in 1984. In 1985, he married Elaine Gaston, originally from the Detroit area. They decided to plant their roots in Minneapolis where they found a spiritual home at St Joan of Arc Catholic Church.

Mark and Elaine have been blessed with many friends and supportive communities that have helped them navigate their lives and rebound from some of the adversities and challenges they have faced. Mark found enjoyable work with a plumbing manufacturer, Bennerotte Marketing Company, as he saw how skills in one area could be transferred to other areas.

The life-changing event that took place in 1995, when Mark was confronted with his addictive behaviors, which began his journey with the Twelve Steps by attending a 12-Step group focused on sex addiction. Mark was challenged to begin facing his addiction, and the Wednesday evening group he has attended for almost thirty years became a pivotal part of his recovery. He feels he owes much to this group as well as to the Twelve Steps and the Serenity Prayer.

After his work retirement, Mark has kept active and creative: officiating at weddings and adult softball games, coaching and sponsoring individuals in recovery, serving as a life coach, and ministering at St. Joan of Arc Church. He continues to speak on the topics such as gratitude, resilience, the importance of finding communities that can affirm and support us, and how to incorporate the Twelve Steps as a way of life day by day.

Believing in the importance of dialogue as a way to continue to learn, Mark Scannell would be excited to hear from you.

Please share your insights, feedback, and questions with him at: gasscann@bitstream.net

~

Mark is available as a speaker on the topics such as the importance of developing a regular practice of giving thanks, learning ways to be resilient, finding communities that can affirm and support us, and ways to incorporate the 12 Steps as a way of living life day by day.

He is licensed to officiate at weddings, and he offers his services in helping couples plan their wedding ceremonies.

As a life coach, Mark helps individuals discover what is of true value to them as well as help them identify actions that can help them embody their values.

For any of the above services, contact Mark at:

612.387.3778

email: gasscann@bitstream.net

Books by Mark T. Scannell

The Gratitude Element: A New Look at the Serenity Prayer

Resilience: The Ability to Rebound from Adversity

The Village it Takes: The Power to Affirm

Affirm & Nurture: A New Look at 12 Steps

Made in the USA
Monee, IL
06 August 2024